INTRODUCTION TO GROUP DYNAMICS

INTRODUCTION TO GROUP DYNAMICS

Malcolm and Hulda Knowles

ASSOCIATION PRESS • NEW YORK

ORIENTATION

How NOT to Read This Book

WE OPEN ON A NEGATIVE note for a reason. Too often we ourselves have read simple books on complicated subjects with the false expectation that they would provide a short cut to expertness. We want to avoid any danger that you will be unrealistic about what you can expect to get out of this book.

Our mission in the book is modest, but, we believe, important. It is to paint a panoramic picture, in broad sweeping strokes, of the new and complicated field of group dynamics. Our purpose is to help you see it in perspective and grasp its main ideas. We hope to acquaint you with the language you will find in research reports about group dynamics sufficiently to give you a running start in reading them—for the social scientists use words that are not in the everyday vocabularies of many of us, both because they are describing concepts that are new and because they are trying to be scientifically precise.

We do not propose to try to provide a comprehensive analysis of the findings of the research into group behavior (that would require an encyclopedia). Nor do we set out to provide a manual of practice. This is not a "how to do" book but rather a "how to find out" book.

We hope that you will finish this book feeling that it has opened new horizons for understanding yourself and your fellow man, and wanting to probe the scientific literature that explores these horizons. We'll try to help you get started.

CONTENTS

INTRODUCTION TO GROUP DYNAMICS

Chapter 1

WHAT IS GROUP DYNAMICS?

FIRST, A FEW WORDS about what group dynamics is *not*. Because it is such a new field of study, some misconceptions have arisen about it. One misconception is that it is a well-organized school of thought or cult, with exclusive membership and a program of social action. It is not. Another misconception is that it is a technique or way of doing things. Thus, we have heard people talk about "the group dynamics method" —a phrase that, as we shall see, is really meaningless. A third misconception is that group dynamics is a doctrinaire approach to social organization which advocates "groupthink" over individualism. Nothing could be farther from the truth.

Four Uses of the Term

If group dynamics is not these things, then what is it? The term has come to be used in four different ways:

1. In its most basic sense, it is used to describe something that is happening in all groups at all times, whether anyone is aware of it or not.

"Group dynamics" used in this way refers to the complex forces that are acting upon every group throughout its existence which cause it to behave the way it does. We can think of every group as having certain relatively static aspects —its name, constitutional structure, ultimate purpose, and other fixed characteristics. But it also has *dynamic* aspects—it is always moving, doing something, changing, becoming, interacting, and reacting. And the nature and direction of its movement is determined by forces being exerted on it from within itself and from outside. The interaction of these forces and their resultant effects on a given group constitute its dynamics. In this sense, "group dynamics" is to groups what "personality dynamics" is to individuals. It is a phenomenon that occurs naturally; nobody invents it.

2. "Group dynamics" is also used to describe a field of study—a branch of the social sciences concerned with using scientific methods to determine why groups behave the way they do. In this sense, it is possible to speak of "the investigation of group dynamics" in the same way that it is possible to speak of "the investigation of nuclear energy." As a field of study, group dynamics employs the tools and personnel of several disciplines of the social sciences: notably social psychology, clinical psychology, psychi-

atry, sociology, anthropology, and education. It makes use of the research facilities of a number of universities. It includes in its field of study the phenomena that occur in groups in industry, the military services, educational institutions, voluntary organizations, social agencies, and in local communities. It sets up hypotheses and then tests them, using such techniques as observation of laboratory and natural groups, interviews, questionnaires, and various kinds of tests. From its factual findings it seeks to develop classifications of group phenomena, theories, and general principles.

3. A third use of the phrase is in reference to the body of basic knowledge about group behavior that has accumulated from past research. It is in this sense that one would speak of "the findings of group dynamics." This body of knowledge is found in doctoral dissertations, articles in the journals of the social sciences, monographs, pamphlets, and a growing number of technical books.

4. Finally, "group dynamics" has come to be used to describe a growing body of *applied* knowledge, or technology, which attempts to translate the findings and theories of basic knowledge into practical principles and methods. Applied group dynamics is concerned with the use of knowledge about group processes. In this sense,

it is possible to speak of "group dynamics principles" or "techniques based on group dynamics," but never of "the group dynamics method."
There is, of course, a close relationship between
basic and applied knowledge. As Kurt Lewin
pointed out in 1944, "In the field of group dynamics, more than in any other psychological
field, are theory and practice linked methodo-
logically in a way which, if properly handled,
could provide answers to theoretical problems
and at the same time strengthen that rational
approach to our practical social problems which
is one of the basic requirements of their solution."[*1] Nevertheless, in trying to understand
group dynamics it is necessary to distinguish between the body of basic knowledge and the
technology which is derived from it. It is important to realize, also, that the principles and
techniques derived from it do not proceed from
an ideological position regarding how groups
ought to behave; rather, they grow out of scientific evidence that certain types of behavior
under certain conditions produce predictable
consequences. Thus, the literature of applied
group dynamics ideally does not say, "Do this
or that," but rather, "If you do so and so under

---

* All footnotes and documentations appear at the end of the
book under "Notes by Chapters."

certain conditions, such and such is likely to happen."

Historical Perspective

The group has always been an important means for the accomplishment of human purposes. First in the family, then the clan, the tribe, the guild, the community, and the state, groups have been used as instruments of government, work, fighting, worship, recreation, and education. Very early in this historical development men began to discover by trial and error that certain ways of doing things in groups worked better than others, and so a body of folk wisdom began to accumulate regarding the selection of leaders, the division of labor, procedures for making decisions, and other group techniques. It is natural that in an era of struggle against natural and human enemies the major concern was with assuring disciplined subservience to leadership rather than with improving the ability of group members to work together creatively and co-operatively.

In view of the fact that man has worked with small groups during most of his life on earth, it is indeed surprising that groups have received virtually no scholarly attention until modern times. Most of the fleeting notice given the subject in earlier literature consisted either of the expression of intuitive ideas, as in the writings of Lao-Tse, or of the didactic listing of rules for leaders to use in manipulating their subjects, as in Machiavelli's *The Prince*.

It seems almost an inversion of normal processes that man did not begin to study seriously the small group life with which he is most intimately familiar until after he had devoted centuries of thought to the larger, more remote aspects of social organization. Moral philosophers beginning with the ancient Chinese and Greeks have been concerned with phenomena associated with the behavior of large collections of people. Beginning late in the seventeeth century there developed a stream of speculative thinking about the social nature of man and the relationship between individuals and collectivities that laid the intellectual foundation for the revolutions against tyranny that swept through Europe and America during the next two centuries. This speculative stream included such Europeans as Hobbes, Locke, Hume, Mill, Smith, Montesquieu, and Rousseau, and such Americans as Madison, Paine, Jefferson, and John and Samuel Adams.

The early sociologists, beginning with Comte and Spencer and their followers in the nineteenth century, narrowed the scope of speculation to the crowd, the mob, the public, and mass movements, with their attendant phenomena of fads, fashions, hysteria, and the like. One of the most influential lines of thought was developed by the French sociologist, Emile Durkheim, around the turn of the century. He became especially interested in the process of interaction and theorized that individual ideas are altered in the process of "psyche-social synthesis" that goes on in groups, and that thus a group product emerges that cannot be explained in terms of individual mental processes.

In the early part of the twentieth century Cooley, Mead, and Simmel speculated about the element of social control in small groups, with special interest in the social conditions under which the motivation of individuals is most effectively developed. Hare, Borgatta, and Bales point out that the theme of the social control of behavior also dominated most of the early experimental research, and go on to summarize this research as follows:

"Among the earliest relevant experimental studies are those of Tripplett in 1898, concerned with a curious facilitating or 'dynamogenic' effect that occurred when people were together and in competition rather than alone. The alone and together theme was given a new impetus in the early twenties by the experiments of F. H. Allport, and is still active today. The study of child development by first-hand observation is another important source of small group research which goes back at least to the turn of the century. . . . Terman's 1904 study of the 'Psychology and Pedagogy of Leadership' among children . . . is classic in its foreshadowing of methods and themes that were to be developed later in the work of Goodenough, Anderson, D. S. Thomas, Pigors, and many others. Piaget's work on children's games is almost in a class by itself as an exemplification of the study of the small group as the creator and carrier of a sub-culture."[2]

In the early 1920's Eduard Lindeman challenged the speculative character of most of the sociological studies of the group and suggested an empirical method for the study of functional groups. Under this stimulus the first large-scale attempt to do research on group process was carried on in "The Inquiry," which is reported in Lindeman's *Social Education*. The interest of "The Inquiry" focused on processes used by small deliberative committees and conferences in the solution of large social problems.

Benne and Levit provide us with this concise summary of other research in the 1920's:

"Under the influence of Dewey's analysis of the act of experimental thought, students of discussion groups and discussion method developed a conception of group process as problem-solving, and developed descriptions and prescriptions for effective group procedure around this central concept. Elliott and Sheffield are representative of this emphasis. . . .

"Motivated by the same psychological and logical currents as Lindeman and Dewey, Follett, through her extensive work in diagnosing current human problems in political, social-welfare, and industrial settings, came to identify the quality, character, and conditions of participation as the focus for studies of group process and experience. Her emphasis on leadership of function, as opposed to leadership of position or personality, and her stress on integrative behavior as a way of resolving conflicts creatively have exerted continuing influence on both study and practice of group methods. . . .

"In addition to these logical and psychological influences upon group studies in the 1920's, Freud began a continuing line of inquiry into group formation and control. Drawing from the intimate and frequently unconscious bases of cohesion and control in the family group, Freud stressed the emotional aspects of group leadership and group formation rather than the organization of members for conscious work.

"Somewhat apart from these theoretical reorientations toward group study, more or less isolated empirical studies of particular groups or kinds of groups went on during the 1920's without much attention to the demands of any comprehensive theory or of theorizing as a component to the research. Kolb's attempt to characterize rural groups represented such empirical investigations from a sociological slant. And Watson's demonstration that groups are more effective than individuals in solving certain types of problems was an example of such early group studies on the psychological side."[3]

A large volume of fact-finding studies based on the "trait theory" of leadership was also spawned in this era of "empiricist rebellion." A number of investigators sought evidence in support of the theory that certain personality traits (such as self-control, common sense, judgment, justice, enthusiasm, tact, perseverance, courage, decisiveness) are common to all successful leaders. This line of study produced a large volume of data, but few conclusions, because there was little agreement on the common traits. Charles Bird analyzed about one hundred such studies and found that only five per cent of the traits mentioned were common to four or more investigations.[4] Other investigators, employing the tools of sociology, sought to discover *ideal types* of leaders for different situations or social structures, such as bureaucracies, labor unions, political parties, and the like. This line of investigation established the importance of situational factors but was not otherwise especially fruitful.

The Modern Era

The modern era in the scientific study of group behavior began to take decisive shape in the early 1930's with the emergence of the more or less integrated theoretical approaches described in the next section. This era has several notable characteristics.

One characteristic is the establishment of a number of research centers focusing specifically on group phenomena, of which the following are examples:

Research Center for Group Dynamics, University of Michigan

Social Relations Laboratory, Harvard University.

Research Center for Human Relations, New York University

Human Dynamics Laboratory, University of Chicago

Human Relations Center, Boston University

Center for Improving Group Procedures, Columbia University

Fels Group Dynamics Laboratory, University of Delaware

Group Dynamics Center, Temple University

Ohio State University Leadership Studies

Laboratory of Personality Assessment and Group Behavior, University of Illinois

Many of these centers practice team research in which specialists from various disciplines collaborate. In addition, many individual scholars in most of the leading universities of the country have become deeply engaged in research in this field.

Another characteristic of the modern era is the rapidly increasing volume of technical literature. At least three quarterly journals are devoted almost exclusively to reporting basic and applied research studies—*The Journal of Social Issues, Human Relations,* and *Sociometry.* The journals of the social science disciplines have given an increasing amount of space to similar scientific reports. Outstanding among these are: *Journal of Applied Psychology, Journal of Abnormal and Social Psychology, Psychological Review, Journal of Social Psychology, American Journal of Sociology, American Sociological Review, Applied Anthropology, Harvard Business Review, Personnel,* and *Journal of Educational Research.* One periodical, *Adult Leadership,* has given major attention to the technology of group dynamics, and numerous articles of this type have appeared in other organizational magazines. The list of book titles, of which the readings contained in the last chapter are but a small sample, has been growing with equal acceleration. A rising number of books and pamphlets of the "how to do" variety have also begun to appear.

A third characteristic of the modern era is the growth of training programs—laboratories, workshops, institutes, seminars—many of which combine research and training. This technological aspect of group dynamics is described in Chapter 4.

Different Approaches to the Study of Groups

Cartwright and Zander aptly describe the current status of the literature of group dynamics in these words:

"As one studies the various writings about groups, one is impressed with the multitude of different ways in which problems have been stated, the great variety of research methods that have been employed, and the confusion of tongues in describing what happens in groups. A first reaction might well be to become disheartened by the apparent chaos and disagreement. A more careful study of the field will reveal, however, that many of the apparently competing 'theories' and 'explanations' do not actually contradict but rather augment and amplify one another."[5]

The apparent confusion in the literature is partly the result of the many different kinds of groups used for research—school classes, factory production teams, jet bomber crews, and fabricated laboratory groups are illustrative of the range. Partly the confusion stems from the diversity of social problems that have motivated research, ranging from intergroup conflict to factory production. And partly it is a product of the interdisciplinary character of the field, with its ideas, methods, and terminology consisting of a potpourri drawn from psychology, sociology, psychiatry, anthropology, industrial relations, social work, education, speech, a pinch of political science and economics, and even a frequent dash of mathematics and physical science.

But more fundamental than these differences are the

variations in theoretical approaches to the study of groups. It will help in understanding the literature of group dynamics to have an overview of the principal approaches currently in vogue.

THE FIELD THEORETICAL APPROACH

The foundation for a "field theory" of group behavior was laid by Kurt Lewin, who came to this country in 1932 as a visiting lecturer at Stanford and remained in this country when the Nazi coup made his return to Berlin impossible. In 1935 Lewin and a dedicated group of graduate students initiated a series of classic studies of group behavior at the University of Iowa's Child Welfare Research Station. This group moved in the midforties to the Massachusetts Institute of Technology to form the Research Center for Group Dynamics. Within a year after Lewin's death in 1947 the Center moved again, to the University of Michigan. This Center has exerted a powerful influence on the study of group dynamics through its field theoretical approach.

Field theory, which has been so productive in physics, makes the assumption that a group at any point of time exists in a psychological field that operates not unlike an electromagnetic field in physics. This field consists of a number of forces (or variables) that are affecting the behavior of the group. The direction and relative strength of these forces determine the direction and speed of movement of the group. It is the task of the social scientist to develop techniques of observation and measurement that will enable him to analyze these forces and state the laws governing their operation. According to Lewin:

"What is important in field theory is the way the analysis proceeds. Instead of picking out one or another isolated element within a situation, the importance of which cannot be judged without consideration of the situation as a whole, field theory finds it advantageous, as a rule, to start with the characterization of the situation as a whole. After this first approximation, the various aspects and parts of the situation undergo a more and more specific and detailed analysis. It is obvious that such a method is the best safeguard against being misled by one or another element of the situation."[6]

Lewin felt that it was especially important to make mathematical representations of psychological situations so as to assure strictness of logic, power of analysis, and conceptual precision. Accordingly, his writings and those of his followers are liberally sprinkled with mathematical formulae and geometric figures.

Some of the research studies conducted under the field theory that might help to convey its spirit are these:

"An Experimental Study of the Effect of Democratic and Authoritarian Group Atmospheres," by R. Lippitt. *University of Iowa Studies in Child Welfare*, 1940, XVI, No. 3, 43.

"The Disruption and Cohesion of Groups," by J. R. P. French, Jr. *Journal of Abnormal and Social Psychology*, 1941, XXXVI, 361.

"Some Effects of Power on the Relations Among Group Members," by J. L. Hurwitz, A. F. Zander, and B. Hymovitch. Cartwright and Zander, *Group Dynamics Research and Theory*, 483.

THE FACTOR ANALYSIS APPROACH

Exemplified by the work of Raymond Cattell and his associates at the University of Illinois, this approach seeks to determine the major dimensions of groups by identifying their key elements. "That is to say," according to Cattell, "one would measure a large number of groups on a large number of attributes and determine a decidedly more limited number of independent dimensions by which any particular group in a given population of groups could be most economically and functionally defined."[7] He uses the term "syntality" to define for the group what "personality" defines for the individual. He is especially concerned with the factors of energy, ability, and leadership.

Examples of studies employing this approach include:

"The Dimensions of Syntality in Small Groups," by R. B. Cattell, D. R. Saunders, and G. F. Stice. *Human Relations*, 1953, VI, 331.

"The Dimensions of Culture Patterns by Factorization of National Character," by R. B. Cattell. *Journal of Abnormal and Social Psychology*, 1949, XLIV, 443.

"The Emergence of Leadership in Small Temporary Groups of Men," by C. A. Gibb. Unpublished doctor's dissertation, University of Illinois, 1949.

THE FORMAL ORGANIZATION APPROACH

Concerned primarily with developing a satisfactory conception of organization and an understanding of the nature of leadership in formal organizations, this approach has dominated the research conducted over a period of years by the Ohio State University Leadership Studies staff headed by C. L. Shartle. Its techniques emphasize observations of interactions in organizational systems and detailed descriptions of the formal organizational structure of the systems. Examples of studies using this approach include:

"Situational Factors in Leadership," by J. K. Hemphill. *Ohio State University Bureau of Educational Research Monographs*, 1949, No. 35.

"Leadership and Executive Performance," by C. L. Shartle. *Personnel*, 1949, XXV, 370.

"Methods for Determining Patterns of Leadership

Behavior in Relation to Organization Structure and Objectives," by R. M. Stogdill and C. L. Shartle. *Journal of Applied Psychology*, 1948, XXXII, 286.

THE SOCIOMETRIC APPROACH

Developed by the psychiatrist, J. L. Moreno, and his early associate, Helen Jennings, this approach focuses on the social aspects of group life, especially the emotional quality of the interpersonal relationships among group members. The method that lies at the heart of this approach is the sociometric test, in which the group members indicate which of the other group members they would choose or not choose as friends, partners, teammates, and the like, in particular situations. The development of the psychological structure of groups can be traced from data obtained from sociometric tests. This approach has produced such studies as these:

"The Social Interrelations of Strangers and Acquaintances," by R. G. Barker. *Sociometry*, 1942, V, 169.

"Statistics of Social Configurations," by J. L. Moreno and H. H. Jennings. *Sociometry*, 1938, I, 342.

"Social Attraction-Patterns in a Village," by G. A. Lunberg and M. Steele. *Sociometry*, 1938, I, 375.

THE INTERACTION ANALYSIS APPROACH

Pioneered by Robert F. Bales and his colleagues at the Harvard University Social Relations Laboratory, this approach asserts that the overt behavior of individuals in interaction with one another and their environment is the "ultimate stuff" of scientific study. Elaborate devices, including an electrical "interaction recorder," and laboratory rooms with one-way windows so that groups can be observed without disturbance, have been invented for measuring interaction in small groups. Some studies produced under this approach include:

> "Phases in Group Problem Solving," by R. F. Bales and F. L. Strodbeck. *Journal of Abnormal and Social Psychology*, 1951, XLVI, 485.
>
> "Power Relations in Three-Person Groups," by T. M. Mills. In Cartwright and Zander, *op. cit.*, 428.
>
> "A Set of Categories for the Analysis of Small Group Interaction," by R. F. Bales. *American Sociological Review*, 1950, XV, 257.

THE PSYCHOANALYTIC APPROACH

The emotional—primarily unconscious—elements in the group process and their effects on personality growth are stressed in this approach. Its method consists chiefly of the analysis of carefully recorded experiences and case records. This approach deals largely, although by no means exclusively, with therapeutic groups. Studies resulting from this approach include:

"Group Emotion and Leadership," by F. Redl. *Psychiatry*, 1942, V, 573.

"A Psychoanalytic Approach to Group Treatment," by H. A. Ezriel. *British Journal of Medical Psychology*, 1950, XXIII, 59.

"The Three-Dimensional Basis of Emotional Interactions in Small Groups," by F. K. Taylor. *Human Relations*, 1954, VII, 441.

THE SOCIAL GROUP WORK APPROACH

This approach has traditionally consisted of the analysis of narrative records of group workers and the extracting of generalizations from series of case histories of groups. Social group work has been primarily concerned with personality development through group experience, although not in a therapeutic setting. Group workers have tended to be more interested in practice than in research, and so the volume of scientifically validated studies from this approach has not been great. In recent years there has been a shift in group work research from descriptive research to action-research "to ascertain the influence of the leader's behavior and other conditions on the interaction within the group and on the personality development of its members."[8] Titles in this branch of the literature include:

"Therapy Through Social Group Work," by G. Konopka. *Proceedings of the National Conference of Social Work*, 1946.

"Some Factors of Resistance Which Affect Group Participation," by H. Osborn. *The Group*, XI, No. 2, 1949.

Group Experience and Democratic Values, by Grace Coyle. (New York: Whiteside, Inc., 1947).

These are the chief approaches or theoretical orientations in the study of group dynamics, as seen by the authors. The names given to them are merely descriptive of the primary characteristic that differentiates them from other approaches. It is important to realize, however, that these are not highly organized, rigidly defined, exclusive schools of thought that are at war with one another. Quite the contrary, there is much intercommunication and co-operation among them. Each makes use of ideas and techniques of the others. Many social scientists would resist being classified strictly in one approach or another, on the score that they make use of the best tools and concepts of all of them.

Succeeding chapters will attempt to describe some of the main ideas about group behavior that have emerged, without further concern for distinguishing between the various approaches. But in trying to understand the literature of group dynamics it is helpful to know that there are these differences in theory, method, focus, and language.

Chapter 2

UNDERSTANDING INDIVIDUAL BEHAVIOR

GROUPS ARE, FIRST OF ALL, collections of individuals. An understanding of the behavior of groups, therefore, has to start with an understanding of the behavior of individuals. Much of the research about group dynamics is concerned with gaining a better understanding of the causes and dynamics of individual behavior in groups, and students of group dynamics make abundant use of findings about individual behavior from related sciences, especially clinical psychology and psychiatry.

Where would a person who wants to understand the different kinds of variable forces that cause individuals to behave the way they do in groups start his inquiry? The starting point, it seems to us, is to know what questions to ask and then to know where to go in the literature of the social sciences to find answers. We'll try to provide a general study guide.

Life History Forces

One set of questions one must ask has to do with the effect of an individual's past experiences in life. The findings of psychoanalytic research are an especially rich source of answers in this line of inquiry. They suggest that the attitudes, values, and habits developed in the first group in a person's life, the family, may strongly influence his feelings and behavior toward leaders and authorities and toward other group members. He may act out in a group the drama of his family life—he may be either submissive or rebellious to a parent-figure, either a rival or a companion to brothers and sisters, and he may feel most at home in either a warm and co-operative atmosphere or one that is cold and antagonistic. In other groups to which he has belonged during his lifetime he has also learned responses and behavior. If a certain pattern of behavior brought the desired results or was comfortable in previous groups, he will tend to repeat that pattern.

This area of research also indicates that one effect of past experience is the development of certain fairly stable tendencies to respond to similar situations in consistent ways. For example, out of the theoretical work by Bion and the further research by Stock and Thelen comes the notion that personality tendencies (termed "valencies") especially relevant to group behavior include "fight, flight, pairing, and dependency":

". . . an individual who has a strong valency for fight tends to express hostility freely in the group; a strong valency for pairing indicates a tendency to express warmth freely and to wish to establish close relationships with others; a strong valency for dependency indicates a tendency to rely on others for support and direction; and a strong valency for flight indicates a tendency to avoid, in some way, the interactive situation. Every person possesses some valency, in varying degrees, for each of these emotional modalities. Such tendencies reside in the individual and form part of an habitual or stable approach to group interaction."[1]

Forces Based on Psychological Needs

Another type of forces to which much research is directed is what is often depicted as universal needs. The biological needs, such as food, water, rest, activity, sex, are widely acknowledged. Less well understood are the psychological needs that are common to all human beings, which are the targets of a good deal of research by psychologists and anthropologists. Although these needs are often given varying labels, they include such ideas as the need for security, the need for affection or response, the need for status or recognition, for belonging, for new experience, and so on. These needs are not of the same strength for all people, nor for one person at different points of time; each individual has his own unique pattern of needs at a given moment. Furthermore, there is a presumption that a given need may express itself in quite different types of behavior by different individuals or by the same individual in different situations. For example, every individual on entering a new group has a need for security about what is expected of him. In one instance this need might result in withdrawal or holding back until the new member gets his bearings. In another instance the need for security might result in the opposite behavior of protective over-talkativeness.

An important insight that comes from the study of psychological needs is that they are not appropriate subjects for moral judgment. It makes as much sense to blame a person for needing recognition as it does to blame him for being hungry when his stomach is empty. If his need for recognition is causing him to irritate the group by monopolizing the discussion or other attention-getting behavior, the fault is not in his needing recognition—we all need it—but in his not knowing how to get it in socially acceptable ways. This area of research does not suggest that laymen should go around making off-the-cuff diagnoses of other individuals' psychological needs. But by understanding that all behavior is caused, the way is opened for us to become more tolerant and accepting of other people's actions and thereby to react to them constructively rather than with irritation and rejection.

Associational Forces

Another set of forces influencing the individual's behavior is induced by what we might think of as his "invisible committees." Every person is associated with a multiplicity of population groupings, some by intent but many by no act of will. Some may be unorganized and vaguely defined—we are business men or workers, housewives or teachers, Negro or white, Protestants, Catholics, or Jews, Democrat, Republican, or Independent. Others may be more definite and specific —our family, our neighborhood, the League of Women Voters, the YMCA, the First Methodist Church, the Centerville Chamber of Commerce, the United Steel Workers, and so on. In a sense, every time an individual starts to make a move several invisible committees representing these affiliations are sitting behind him putting pressure on him to act in certain ways—indeed, often in conflicting ways. And when he acts, it is with the feeling that whatever he does is being judged by these "reference groups" according to their purposes, standards, values, and goals.

Forces from Goals and Ideologies

Another set of forces influencing an individual's behavior is tending to pull him rather than push him. These forces are his own goals, his own standards and values, his own perceptions of reality, his own fears, his own conceptions of what he is and wants to be. Though these forces have grown out of all the other influences in his life, they have been given a unique shape in the way he has put them together. They are the magnets of his private world. And when the chips are down, they may well be the most influential factor of all in determining his behavior. Some research suggests that when a situation permits a person to be himself—to act freely and with integrity—his behavior will be the most constructive and creative of which he is capable. It is when he is under goading pressures to be something other than what he is—to be alienated from himself—that he is likely to become a "problem personality." The writings of Erich Fromm and David Riesman are especially illuminating in this area of investigation.

This is, of course, an oversimplified picture of the personality dynamics of an individual. But it may serve as a provocation, if not an enticement, to dip more deeply into the scientific literature on individual behavior. You will want to explore at least two additional lines of inquiry: (1) What are the effects of the dynamic interplay of these forces on one another? (2) What is the role of the symbolic processes—reasoning, planning, intending, imagining, thinking—in producing behavior? And you will no doubt want to look for other types of forces omitted from this brief overview.

To summarize, the types of forces at work on an individual as he enters a group that are depicted in the psychological literature might be pictured graphically somewhat like this:

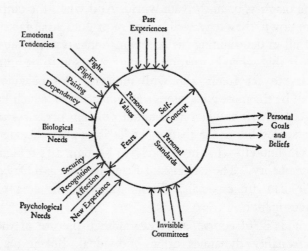

A full reading of the scientific literature along these lines of inquiry would not, however, provide a complete explanation of member behavior in groups, for there are some distinctly *group* variables which must also be taken into account, and on these we next turn our spotlight.

Chapter 3

UNDERSTANDING GROUP BEHAVIOR

A LEGITIMATE QUESTION to raise at this point is this: what happens when one individual, with his psychological field, gets together with other individuals with their unique psychological fields? How do they become a group, with its own unitary psychological field?

What Is a Group?

The writers in the field of group dynamics do not agree completely on what distinguishes those collections of individuals that are groups from those that are not. But most of their disagreements are in emphasis and terminology. In general, they agree that a collection of people is a group when it possesses these qualities:

1. A definable membership—a collection of two or more people identifiable by name or type.
2. Group consciousness—the members think of themselves as a group, have a "collective perception of unity," a conscious identification with each other.

3. A sense of shared purpose—the members have the same "object model" or goals or ideals.

4. Interdependence in satisfaction of needs—the members need the help of one another to accomplish the purposes for which they joined the group.

5. Interaction—the members communicate with one another, influence one another, react to one another.

6. Ability to act in a unitary manner—the group can behave as a single organism.

The essential differences between a collection of individuals that is a group and one that is not might be portrayed graphically like this:

A COLLECTION OF INDIVIDUALS   A GROUP

In the collection that is not a group there are no shared goals—the goal arrows of the various individuals are pointing in different directions; there is no boundary around the collection, indicating a lack of consciousness as a group and undefinable membership;

there are no lines of interaction and interdependence connecting the individuals; and obviously the collection is unable to act in a unitary manner.

Some Properties of Groups

There is such a profusion of kinds of groups in our nation of joiners that there appear to be few similarities among them. We can all name many groups to which we belong—the family, our social circle, the people we work with (and those special friends we go with on the coffee break), the infinite variety of committees we serve on at church, school, the club, the union, and in the community; and hopefully some study groups at the library, the Y, or the high school or college. In studying groups of all these types the researchers have identified certain properties or characteristics that all groups possess. These are the properties most commonly investigated and described:

1. *Background.* Each group has an historical background—or lack of it—which influences its behavior. A new group coming together for the first time may have to devote much of its early energy to getting acquainted with one another and with the group's task, as well as establishing ways of working together. On the other hand, a group that has met together often may be assumed to be better acquainted with what to expect from one another, what needs to be done, and how to do it. But it might also have developed habits

that interfere with its efficiency, such as arguing, dividing into factions, or wasting time.

Members come into a meeting with some expectations about it. They may have a clear idea of what the meeting is about, or they may be hazy and puzzled about what is going to happen. They may be looking forward to the meeting or dreading it; they may feel deeply concerned or indifferent. In some cases the boundaries around the group's freedom of action may be narrowly defined by the conditions under which it was created, or so poorly defined that the group doesn't know what its boundaries are.

These are merely illustrations of some of the elements that make up a group's background. Some questions that help to provide an understanding of a group's background include:

> How well were the members prepared to enter the group?
>
> What are their expectations about the group and their role in it?
>
> What is the composition of the group—what kind of people, what is their previous experience, prior friendship patterns, and so on? How were they selected?
>
> What arrangements have been made for their meeting—physical setting, resources, and the like?

2. *Participation pattern.* At any given moment every group has a particular participation pattern. For

instance, it may be all one-way, with the leader talking to the members; or it may be two-way, with the leader speaking to the members and the members responding to him; or it may be multidirectional, with all members speaking to one another and to the group as a whole. In a given group this pattern may tend to be quite consistent, or it may vary from time to time. The studies do not indicate that any one participation pattern is always best; it depends upon the requirements of a given situation. But many studies show that on the whole, the broader the participation among members of a group the deeper the interest and involvement will be.

Some questions you may ask about a group to understand its participation pattern are these:

How much of the talking is done by the leader, how much by the other members?

To whom are questions or comments usually addressed—the group as a whole, the leader, or particular members?

Do the members who don't talk much seem to be interested and listening alertly (nonverbal participation), or are they bored and apathetic?

It is very easy, and often useful to a group, to chart the participation pattern during periodic segments of time, thus providing objective data about this aspect of its dynamics, like this:

PARTICIPATION PATTERN
FROM 8:00 P.M. TO 8:20 P.M.

PARTICIPATION PATTERN
FROM 9:00 P.M. TO 9:20 P.M.

3. *Communication.* This property has to do with how well group members are understanding one another—how clearly they are communicating their ideas, values, and feelings. If some members are using a highly specialized vocabulary they may be talking over the heads of the rest of the group. Sometimes a group will develop a specialized vocabulary of its own, a kind of verbal shorthand, or private jokes that aren't understood by new members and outsiders.

Even nonverbal communication can often be eloquent. A person's posture, facial expression, and gestures, tell a great deal about what he is thinking and feeling.

Some questions that indicate the quality of a group's communications are these:

Are members expressing their ideas clearly?
Do members frequently pick up contributions previously made and build their own ideas on to them?

Do members feel free to ask for clarification when they don't understand a statement?

Are responses to statements frequently irrelevant?

4. *Cohesion.* The cohesiveness of a group is determined by the strength of the bonds that bind the individual parts together into a unified whole. This property indicates the morale, the team spirit, the strength of attraction of the group for its members, and the interest of the members in what the group is doing. In the literature it is often referred to as the "we-feeling" of a group. Symptoms of low cohesion include *sub rosa* conversations between pairs of members outside the main flow of the group's discussion, the emergence of cliques, factions, and such subgroupings as the "old timers" versus the "newcomers," the "conservatives" versus the "liberals," and so on.

Questions about the group's cohesion include:

How well is the group working together as a unit?

What subgroups or "lone wolves" are there and how do they affect the group?

What evidence is there of interest or lack of interest on the part of members or groups of members in what the group is doing?

Do members refer to the group as "my group," "our group," "your group," "their group," or "his group"?

5. *Atmosphere.* Although atmosphere is an intangible thing, it is usually fairly easy to sense. In the

literature it is often referred to as the "social climate" of the group, with such characterizations as "warm, friendly, relaxed, informal, permissive, free," in contrast to "cold, hostile, tense, formal, restrained." Atmosphere affects how members feel about a group and the degree of spontaneity in their participation.

Atmosphere can be probed by such questions as these:

Would you describe this group as warm or cool, friendly or hostile, relaxed or tense, informal or formal, permissive or controlled, free or inhibited?

Can opposing views or negative feelings be expressed without fear of punishment?

6. *Standards.* Every group tends to develop a code of ethics or set of standards about what is proper and acceptable behavior. Which subjects may be discussed, which are taboo; how openly members may express their feelings; the propriety of volunteering one's services; the length and frequency of statements considered allowable; whether or not interrupting is permitted—all these and many more "do's and don'ts" are embodied in a group's standards. It may be difficult for a new member to catch on to a group's standards if they differ from those of other groups he has experienced, since these standards are usually implicit rather than openly stated. Indeed, a group might be confused about what its standards actually are, and

this may lead to much embarrassment, irritation, and lost momentum.

Questions about standards include:

What evidence is there that the group has a code of ethics regarding such matters as self-discipline, sense of responsibility, courtesy, tolerance of differences, freedom of expression, and the like?

Are there any marked deviations from these standards by one or more members? With what effect?

Do these standards seem to be well understood by all members, or is there confusion about them?

Which of the group's standards seem to help, and which seem to hinder the group's progress?

7. *Sociometric pattern.* In every group the participants tend very soon to begin to identify certain individuals that they like more than other members, and others that they like less. These subtle relationships of friendship and antipathy—the sociometric patterns—have an important influence on the group's activities. There is some research that indicates that people tend to agree with people they like and to disagree with people they dislike, even though both express the same ideas.

Questions which help to reveal the sociometric pattern are these:

Which members tend to identify with and support one another?

Which members seem repeatedly at odds?

Do some members act as "triggers" to others, causing them to respond immediately after the first members' comments, either pro or con?

8. *Structure and organization.* Groups have both a visible and an invisible organizational structure. The visible structure, which might be highly formal (officers, committees, appointed positions) or quite informal, makes it possible to achieve a division of labor among the members and get essential functions performed. The invisible structure consists of the behind-the-scenes arrangement of the members according to relative prestige, influence, power, seniority, ability, persuasiveness, and the like.

Questions to ask about structure include:

What kind of structure does the group create consciously—leadership positions, service positions, committees, teams?

What is the invisible structure—who really controls, influences, volunteers, gets things done; who defers to others, follows?

Is the structure understood and accepted by the members?

Is it appropriate to the group's purpose and tasks?

9. *Procedures.* All groups need to use some procedures—ways of working—to get things done. In formal business meetings we are accustomed to the use of *Robert's Rules of Order*, a highly codified and

explicit set of procedures. Informal groups usually use much less rigid procedures. The choice of procedures has a direct effect on such other aspects of group life as atmosphere, participation pattern, and cohesion. Choosing procedures that are appropriate to the situation and to the work to be done requires a degree of flexibility and inventiveness by a group.

Procedures can be examined through such questions as these:

How does the group determine its tasks or agenda?

How does it make decisions—by vote, silent assent, consensus?

How does it discover and make use of the resources of its members?

How does it co-ordinate its various members, subgroups, and activities?

How does it evaluate its work?

10. *Goals.* All groups have goals, some very long-range—for example, "to promote the welfare of children and youth"; others of shorter range—"to plan a parent education program for the coming year"; and others even more immediate—"to decide on a speaker for next month's meeting." Sometimes goals are defined clearly, specifically, and publicly, and other times they are vague, general, and only implicit. Members may feel really committed to them or may merely go along with them. Since goals are so important to the

group's ultimate accomplishment, they receive a good deal of attention in the literature.

Some questions about goals include:

How does the group arrive at its goals?
Are all members clear about them?
Are all members committed to them?
Are they realistic and attainable for this group?

Psyche and Socio Dimensions

The sociometric study of groups has illuminated another aspect of their character which produces further insight about their functioning. In this analysis it appears at first sight that there are two completely different kinds of groups. Some of them, such as the bridge circle, the coffee gang, and the like, are highly informal, with few rules or procedures and no stated goals. People belong to them for the emotional satisfactions they get from belonging; they like the people, they are their friends. They tend to think of these as their social groups, but in the literature they are often called *psyche* groups. Membership in these groups is completely voluntary and tends to be homogeneous. The success of the psyche group is measured in terms of how enjoyable it is.

In other groups, however—committees, boards, staffs, and discussion groups—there are usually explicit goals, and more or less formal rules and procedures. People tend to think of these groups, which exist to accomplish some task, as work or volunteer service groups. But in the language of social science they are *socio* groups. Their membership tends to be more heterogeneous—based on the resources required to do their work—and sometimes brought together out of compulsion or sense of duty more than out of free choice. The success of the socio group is measured in terms of how much work it gets done.

As these dimensions have been studied more deeply it has become apparent that they do not describe different kinds of groups—few groups are purely psyche or socio—so much as different dimensions of all groups. Most groups need the psyche dimension to provide emotional involvement, morale, interest, and loyalty; and the socio dimension to provide stability, purpose, direction, and a sense of accomplishment. Without the dimension of work (socio) members may became dissatisfied and feel guilty because they are not accomplishing anything; without the dimension of friendship (psyche) members may feel that the group is cold, unfriendly, and not pleasant to be with. These dimensions of group life are dealt with most specifically in the writings of Helen Jennings.

Membership and Leadership Functions

Another aspect of group life that is crucial in understanding a group's behavior, diagnosing its problems, and improving its operation, is the way in which various required functions are performed. Kenneth Benne and Paul Sheats developed the following widely used classification of these functions: (1) *group-building and maintenance* roles—those which contribute to building relationships and cohesiveness among the membership (the psyche dimension), and (2) *group task* roles—those which help the group to do its work (the socio dimension). The first set of functions is required for the group to maintain itself as a group; the second set, for the locomotion of the group toward its goals.[1]

For example, some *group-building* functions are these:

Encouraging—being friendly, warm, responsive to others, praising others and their ideas, agreeing with and accepting the contributions of others.

Mediating—harmonizing, conciliating differences in points of view, making compromises.

Gate keeping—trying to make it possible for another member to make a contribution by saying, "We haven't heard from Jim yet," or suggesting limited talking-time for everyone so that all will have a chance to be heard.

Standard setting—expressing standards for the group to use in choosing its subject matter or procedures, rules of conduct, ethical values.

Following—going along with the group, somewhat passively accepting the ideas of others, serving as an audience during group discussion, being a good listener.

Relieving tension—draining off negative feeling by jesting or throwing oil on troubled waters, diverting attention from unpleasant to pleasant matters.

And the following are some *task functions*:

Initiating—suggesting new ideas or a changed way of looking at the group problem or goal, proposing new activities.

Information seeking—asking for relevant facts or authoritative information.

Information giving—providing relevant facts or authoritative information or relating personal experience pertinently to the group task.

Opinion giving—stating a pertinent belief or opinion about something the group is considering.

Clarifying—probing for meaning and understanding, restating something the group is considering.

Elaborating—building on a previous comment, enlarging on it, giving examples.

Co-ordinating—showing or clarifying the relationships among various ideas, trying to pull ideas and suggestions together.

Orienting—defining the progress of the discussion in terms of the group's goals, raising questions about the direction the discussion is taking.

Testing—checking with the group to see if it is ready to make a decision or to take some action.

Summarizing—reviewing the content of past discussion.

These functions are not needed equally at all times by a group. Indeed, if a given function is performed inappropriately it may interfere with the group's operation—as when some jester relieves group tension just when the tension is about to result in some real action. But often when a group is not getting along as it should, a diagnosis of the problem will probably indicate that nobody is performing one of the functions listed above that is needed at that moment to move the group ahead. It seems to be true, also, that some people are more comfortable or proficient in performing one kind of function than another, so that they tend to play the same role in every group to which they belong. There is danger, however, in over-stereotyping an individual as a "mediator" or "opinion giver" or any other particular function, for people can learn to perform various functions that are needed when they become aware of them.

Often in groups one can observe behavior that does not seem to fit any of these categories. This is likely to be *self-centered* behavior, sometimes referred to in the literature as a "nonfunctional role." This is behavior that does not contribute to the group, but only satisfies personal needs. Examples of this category are as follows:

Blocking—interfering with the progress of the group by going off on a tangent, citing personal experiences unrelated to the group's problem, arguing too much on a point the rest of the group has resolved, rejecting ideas without consideration, preventing a vote.

Aggression—criticising or blaming others, showing hostility toward the group or some individual without relation to what has happened in the group, attacking the motives of others, deflating the ego or status of others.

Seeking recognition—attempting to call attention to one's self by excessive talking, extreme ideas, boasting, boisterousness.

Special pleading—introducing or supporting ideas related to one's own pet concerns or philosophies beyond reason, attempting to speak for "the grass roots," "the housewife," "the common man," and so on.

Withdrawing—acting indifferent or passive, resorting to excessive formality, doodling, whispering to others.

Dominating—trying to assert authority in manipulating the group or certain members of it by "pulling rank," giving directions authoritatively, interrupting contributions of others.

The appearance of these behaviors in groups tends to be irritating to other members, and they tend to react to them with blame, reproach, or counterhostility. A group that understands group dynamics is often able to deal with them constructively, however, because it sees them as symptoms of deeper causes, such as valid personal needs that are not being satisfied constructively. Often, of course, it is difficult to place a given act in one or another of these categories —what seems to be "blocking" to one observer may appear as "testing" to another.

The Role of Leadership

In this analysis of functions necessary to the performance of groups no distinction has been made between the functions of leaders and the functions of members. This is because the research fails to identify any set of functions that are *universally* the peculiar responsibility of the designated leader. But the fact is that groups in our society typically have central figures with such titles as "leader," "chairman," "president," and "captain." Ross and Hendry examine various theories that try to explain this institutionalization of the role of leader and, after assessing them as inadequate, give this view as to the current state of thinking:

"Perhaps the best we can say at this point is that any comprehensive theory of leadership must take into account the fact that the leadership role is probably related to personality factors, to the attitudes and needs of 'followers' at a particular time, to the structure of the group, and to the situation. . . . Leadership is probably a function of the interaction of such variables, and these undoubtedly provide for role differentiation which leads to the designation of a 'central figure' or leader, without prohibiting other members in the group from performing leadership functions in various ways, and at various times, in the life of the group."[2]

A classic series of experiments often quoted in the literature of group dynamics bears on leadership style. The experiments were conducted by Ronald Lippitt and Ralph White in the research program headed by Kurt Lewin at the University of Iowa in the 1930's. Their purpose was to measure as precisely as possible the effects of different types of leader behavior on a number of experimentally created groups of boys. The three types of leader behavior tested were "authoritarian" (policy determined by the leader), "democratic" (all policies a matter of group discussion and decision, encouraged and assisted by the leader), and "laissez-faire" (complete freedom for group or individual decision, with a minimum of leader participation). Their studies produced evidence for the following generalizations:

1. Authoritarian-led groups produced a greater quantity of work over a short period of time, but experienced more hostility, competition, and aggression—especially scapegoating, more discontent beneath the surface, more dependence, and less originality.
2. Democratically led groups, slower in getting into

production, were more strongly motivated, became increasingly productive with time and learning, experienced more friendliness and teamwork, praised one another more frequently, and expressed greater satisfaction.

3. Laissez-faire groups did less work and poorer work than either of the others, spent more time in horseplay, talked more about what they should be doing, experienced more aggression than the democratic groups but less than the authoritarian, and expressed a preference for democratic leadership.

A mounting body of research on the leadership role since World War II, especially that sponsored by the Office of Naval Research,[3] supports the thesis that some situations require authoritarian and others laissez-faire leadership, but that in the long run in normal situations groups thrive best when the leadership functions are democratically shared among the members of the group.

Groups in Motion

So far we have been looking at the complicated elements or variables that make up a group—its properties, dimensions, and membership and leadership functions—almost as if a group stood still in time and space. Actually, a group is never static; it is a dynamic organism, constantly in motion. Not only is it moving as a unit, but the various elements within it are constantly interacting. A change in procedure will affect atmosphere, which will affect the participation pattern, which will affect cohesion, which will affect leadership, which will affect procedure, and so on. Actually, most of the research has to do with the dynamic interaction of these variables in groups in motion.

Some General Principles

The study of group dynamics is beginning to produce some generalizations or laws of cause and effect that make it increasingly possible to understand, predict, and improve group behavior. It would be impossible even to try to summarize the body of findings or "working hypotheses" that have accumulated from the research to date in a small book. You might be interested, however, in a sample of the general principles that seem to be emerging.

In this spirit we list below some of the principles that have been most helpful to us in understanding group behavior:

1. A group tends to be attractive to an individual and to command his loyalty to the extent that:
   a. It satisfies his needs and helps him achieve goals that are compelling to him.
   b. It provides him with a feeling of acceptance and security.

  c. Its membership is congenial to him.

  d. It is highly valued by outsiders.

2. Each person tends to feel committed to a decision or goal to the extent that he has participated in determining it.

3. A group is an effective instrument for change and growth in individuals to the extent that:

  a. Those who are to be changed and those who are to exert influence for change have a strong sense of belonging to the same group.

  b. The attraction of the group is greater than the discomfort of the change.

  c. The members of the group share the perception that change is needed.

  d. Information relating to the need for change, plans for change, and consequences of change is shared by all relevant people.

  e. The group provides an opportunity for the individual to practice changed behavior without threat or punishment.

  f. The individual is provided a means for measuring progress toward the change goals.

4. Every force tends to induce an equal and opposite counterforce. (Thus, the preferred strategy for change, other things being equal, is the weakening of forces resisting change rather than the addition of new positive forces toward change. For instance, if a group in a factory is resisting a new work procedure, it may be because they

don't understand how it will work, in which case a demonstration or trial experience will be superior to exhortation or pressure.)

5. Every group is able to improve its ability to operate as a group to the extent that it consciously examines its processes and their consequences and experiments with improved processes. (In the literature this is referred to as the "feedback mechanism," a concept similar to that used in guided missiles, which correct any deviations from their course while in flight on the basis of data collected by sensitive instruments and fed back into their control mechanism.)

6. The better an individual understands the forces influencing his own behavior and that of a group, the better he will be able to contribute constructively to the group and at the same time to preserve his own integrity against subtle pressures toward conformity and alienation.

7. The strength of pressure to conform is determined by the following factors:
   a. The strength of the attraction a group has for the individual.
   b. The importance to the individual of the issue on which conformity is being requested.
   c. The degree of unanimity of the group toward requiring conformity.[4]

8. The determinants of group effectiveness include:
   a. The extent to which a clear goal is present.

b. The degree to which the group goal mobilizes energies of group members behind group activities.

c. The degree to which there is agreement or conflict among members concerning which one of several possible goals should control the activities of the group.

d. The degree to which there is agreement or conflict among the members concerning means that the group should use to reach its goal.

e. The degree to which the activities of different members are co-ordinated in a manner required by the group's tasks.

f. The availability to the group of needed resources, whether they be economic, material, legal, intellectual, or other.

g. The degree to which the group is organized appropriately for its task.

h. The degree to which the processes it uses are appropriate to its task and stage of development.[5]

Chapter 4

PRACTICAL APPLICATIONS

As IS TRUE OF ANY FIELD of fundamental research, many of the findings of research in group dynamics have practical implications. As Thelen states, "The aim of science is to describe nature and its laws. The aim of technology is to state policies by which man can control nature for stated ends. Technology is the set of ideas man uses in acting out his needs and in satisfying his purposes. As science develops and nature is understood better, technology also changes."[1] The fact is that the research into group dynamics has greatly influenced the social technology of working with groups in at least four important areas: (1) leadership (and membership) training, (2) the invention of new techniques, (3) the general spirit or culture of groups and large meetings, and (4) community relations and social change.

Leadership (and Membership) Training

Traditionally, leadership training has consisted of selecting people with the right "traits" for leadership positions and then indoctrinating them with the particular knowledge and skills required for particular jobs, such as being chairmen of particular committees, leading particular types of discussions, teaching particular subjects, or managing particular organizations.

To this dimension of leadership training have been added two new dimensions as a result of the research in group dynamics. The second dimension consists of generalized understandings of group behavior that are applicable to *all* groups in *all* situations. This second dimension might be thought of as the "liberal arts" program in leadership development, whereas the first dimension is more akin to the "vocational training" aspect of leadership development. The third dimension consists of training for all group members, not just the designated leaders, in the skills of group participation. It recognizes that leadership within a group often shifts as situations change and that in many respects the most effective training is done with the group as a whole in terms of its continuous experience.

Major contributions to a new technology of leadership training have been made by a number of centers that specialize in training and research about training. Most of the university centers that are listed on page 21 engage in off-campus training projects on a contractual basis. The American Management Association operates seminars and institutes throughout the country for executive personnel. Both Harvard Business School and the Industrial Relations Center at the Massachusetts Institute of Technology have contributed especially to the development of the case method for training in human relations skills. The Sociometric Institute in Beacon, New York, has advanced the use of psychodramatic and sociometric methods in training.

Perhaps the most widely known, and certainly one of the most productive centers of applied group dynamics, is the National Training Laboratories, which is sponsored by the Division of Adult Education Services of the National Education Association in Washington, D.C. The "NTL" was founded in 1947 by associates of Kurt Lewin, including Kenneth Benne, Leland Bradford, and Ronald Lippitt. It conducts summer "laboratories" varying from one to four weeks in length in Bethel, Maine, to which are drawn leaders from a wide variety of occupations. Since 1951 it has also conducted a year-round consultation program which provides training services for numerous governmental, industrial, and social welfare organizations. Regional laboratories patterned after the Bethel model have sprung up in several other sections of the country.

Building on group dynamics, the "NTL" has broadened its scope to interdisciplinary research and training in the broad field of human behavior. The ideas about theory and methods of training that it has developed have strongly influenced leadership training practices across the country. Members of its staff, drawn from dozens of universities and organizations, have been prolific in their writings and are widely in demand as consultants and workshop leaders, and the hundreds of graduates of its training programs have been influential in carrying ideas back to their organizations and communities.

The new technology of training emphasizes the development of an understanding of the forces at work in groups, the development of sensitivity to the needs of individuals and groups, the development of skill in diagnosing human relations problems, and the development of the ability to learn from actual experience. It starts with the proposition that the target of training is change in the behavior of individuals so that they can take appropriate and effective membership in groups. Bradford explains: "This viewpoint necessitates looking at forces of resistance to change both within the individual and in his total situation as well as at the process of changing. Instead of thinking about ways of 'teaching' facts, it is necessary to analyze the conditions which keep the individual from changing, the requirements to help him change, and the supports necessary to help him maintain his change."[2]

This approach involves the diagnosing of the needs for change, the forces of resistance to change, and the motivations for change in each particular situation, and then designing a training program consisting of a number of elements and using many methods which will help the individual to bring about the changes he desires. Training designs typically make use of the following types of activity:

Laboratory groups. These are given a wide variety of labels, including "T-Groups," "nondirective groups," "diagnostic groups," "sensitivity groups," "workshop groups," and "lab groups." A laboratory group provides participants with the experience of constructing without blueprint or direction an organism which has goals, structure, procedures, standards, and other elements of group life. The trainers do not tell the group what to do, but help them to analyze their behavior as they go about forming a group. In Bradford's words, "The group provides an opportunity for trainees to behave, to secure feed-back on their behavior, to experiment with new ideas of leadership and membership and to get—on the feeling as well as the intellectual level—a real awareness of the problems of group organization, functioning, and growth."[3]

Theory sessions. These are general meetings of all participants in which theories and research findings are presented through lectures, motion pictures, demonstrations, panel discussions, and other methods. Such topics as the following are treated: "Characteristics of Groups," "The New Member in the Group," "Concepts and Kinds of Leadership," "Roles in Effective Group Action," "Understanding Individual Motivation," "Human Factors Affecting Productivity,'

"Problem Solving in Small Groups," "Some Basic Features of Social Systems," and "Communications in Formal Organizations."

Skill practice groups. In these groups the participants actually practice performing various skills of human relations and group participation, through role playing, case method, and other devices. Such skills as these are typically included: diagnosing group problems, being sensitive to the feelings of others and the needs of the group, observing group interaction, performing various member roles flexibly, leading discussions, interviewing, planning meetings and workshops, and the like.

Participative cases. These are in effect mass role-playing exercises in which all participants experience the problems that arise in the relationships among the various kinds of groups in a hypothetical community. A realistic community problem is described (such as whether or not to float a bond issue to build a new community college) in a hypothetical community. Then the learners are assigned to typical community groups that would be concerned with this problem (such as the PTA, the school board, the taxpayers' association, and the like) and they are instructed to act out what they would do to solve the problem. Trained observers collect data about the behavior of the participants as they become absorbed in the project. At the conclusion of the exercise the data are reported, and an analysis is made of what happened and why. Participative cases reinforce laboratory groups in helping people learn how to learn from analyzing their "here and now" behavior.

Project or production groups. Participants gain experience through these groups in planning and carrying out projects for the total laboratory or solving problems in which they are interested. Such projects include publishing a news letter, conducting social events or large meetings, and preparing reports. These groups often provide opportunities to experiment with ways to improve group productivity.

Special-interest groups. Participants choose these groups according to their occupational or functional interests, such as supervision, board operation, staff management, membership recruitment, community organization, public relations, and the like. These groups are usually led by a specialist in the subject and have as their purpose the broadening and deepening of the participants' knowledge of a particular subject.

Application groups. These are small groups, often homogeneous in terms of occupation, geographic location, or institutional affiliation, that plan strategies for transferring their learnings from the laboratory to their back-home situation.

Invention of New Techniques

Because of its emphasis on experimentalism, applied group dynamics has been especially productive of new techniques. Many new techniques have resulted from the desire to find ways to increase and deepen participation and "ego-involvement"—factors discovered to be particularly crucial in group life. In this category can be listed such techniques as listening teams, reaction panels, buzz sessions, problem censuses, group interviews, and the like. In a sense, many of these techniques are an attempt to give large meetings, which occupy such an important place in the American way of life, some of the qualities and advantages of small face-to-face groups.

Another spur to the invention of new techniques has been the discovery of the importance of experience in the learning process. Such techniques as role playing, the case method, nondirective discussion, participative cases, and skill practice exercises, have been developed to provide a way for people to learn from actual experience.

A third major area of technique development has been in data-collection, of which postmeeting reaction forms, sociometric tests, evaluation procedures of various sorts, interaction charts, and the use of process observers, are examples.

Regarding this aspect of applied group dynamics Thelen has these wise words of caution: "A technique is in itself neither good nor bad, but it can be used effectively, with little consequence, or disastrously. Role-playing out of place can be gruesome; buzz grouping when there is nothing to talk about is downright embarrassing; discussion by a panel of 'experts' who have had no experience relevant to the needs of the group is simply maddening; problem censuses before people feel able to formulate their 'real problems' stick them with goals they will reject later; audience listening teams with no opportunity to report back get angry, and so on. I should say that these new techniques should not be assimilated as part of the orthodoxy of a new religion, and they should not stand for 'group dynamics'."[4]

The General Spirit of Groups and Large Meetings

Many of the ideas and techniques resulting from the study of group dynamics have infiltrated into the blood stream of American life and have exerted a subtle influence on the way groups and meetings are conducted. There seems to be a generally more democratic spirit developing in organizational life. An increasing number of groups are employing educational processes along with action processes in order to improve their efficiency and increase their value to their members.[5] In the dozens of meetings we have attended in the last few years, ranging from local PTA's to a national convention of administrators, we can recall only a very few that did not use some device for involving the audience in really active participation—a statement we could not have made even five years ago. And it seems to us that in the numerous meetings of boards, committees, and discussion groups we have observed there has been a noticeable tendency toward shared planning and leadership.

Community Relations and Social Change

A fourth area in which the findings about group dynamics have been applied especially prominently is in the social processes of community life. In the handling of numerous kinds of conflict situations that develop in the normal course of community living—labor-management disputes, race relations, interagency rivalries, and the like—the findings of group dynamics have increasingly been found useful.

Chapter 5

WHAT DOES IT ADD UP TO?

THE FIELD OF GROUP DYNAMICS is too new for anyone to know what its ultimate status in the social sciences will be, or what its full contribution to society
will be. There is some aura of controversy about it
now. Perhaps this is because it is undermining old and
comfortable ways of thinking about groups, or because
of misconceptions about its nature and aims, or because
it is inevitably making some mistakes in the process of
pioneering uncharted territory. Or perhaps the critics
of group dynamics are pointing to fundamental weak-
nesses and errors that need to be corrected. As you
explore the literature of group dynamics, you might
raise some of these questions that are posed by its
critics, to see how it deals with them (we give our
own reactions primarily to clarify the meaning of the
questions, not to prejudice your own search for answers):

*Will the new knowledge and methods being uncov-
ered enable unscrupulous people to manipulate groups
more easily toward their selfish ends?* Most knowledge
can be used for good or evil, just as a sharp axe can be
used either to chop down a tree or to chop off a man's

head. We couldn't ban all new knowledge that might be used for evil without putting a stop to human progress. But in group dynamics there may be two built-in safeguards against this danger: (1) The social scientists themselves are acutely aware of their responsibility to accompany the transmission of new knowledge and skills with ethical undergirding. The literature is rich with examinations of the ethical implications of their work and its relationship to the values of democratic society. And training programs typically include periods for the examination of ethical questions. (2) Two of the essential ingredients of group dynamics training are anti-manipulative in their effect—training in shared leadership and training in the collection and examination of data about what is happening in the group.

Isn't there a danger that all this emphasis on group behavior will lead to a loss of individuality—that "groupthink" will take over? To the social scientists this is almost the "unkindest cut of all." For they know, from their study of groups, that (1) as life becomes increasingly complex individuals become increasingly interdependent and must inevitably do more and more of their work in groups, and (2) nothing can be more tyrannical than a group whose members are unsophisticated about its dynamics. Indeed, probably the best way to preserve individuality is to give every individual the knowledge and skills necessary to diagnose and withstand the forces toward conformity and at the same time to express his individuality constructively. The leaders of group dynamics research and theory have made a special point of trying to disseminate their knowledge widely, and the leaders of applied group dynamics have made a point of training *all* group members, not just selected leaders.

Isn't the group dynamics field focusing too much attention on the process of groups at the expense of the content of their work? Some critics are concerned that groups will become so introspective about their dynamic processes that they will lose sight of their real reasons for being—to produce ideas, pleasures, decisions, or other substantive products. The practitioners of applied group dynamics recognize that there is a danger, especially in the early stages of training, that this new dimension of group life might become so intriguing as to become an end in itself. They have tried to erect safeguards against its happening, including warning against it and pointing it out when it begins to occur. But this is a phenomenon that typically occurs only while people are actually in a training situation. In our experience the greater danger lies in a person's neglecting his newly learned skills of group process observation once he returns home and becomes absorbed in the tasks of the groups to which he belongs.

Will not inexperienced or poorly trained people make use of techniques that might cause damage? Since group dynamics brings into the open the part played by people's feelings in the life of a group, there is some danger that participants in a laboratory group might expose emotions too deep for leaders not trained in psychotherapy to handle. Applied group dynamics recognizes this danger, and builds cautions against it into both its literature and its training programs. Newly trained leaders are urged not to undertake the leadership of laboratory groups until they have served an apprenticeship under careful supervision, and have become skillful in preventing the traumatic overexposure of emotions.

Is there not a tendency for zealots to go "all out" for sensitivity training and to cast off other types of necessary training in specific processes and methods? No doubt such a danger exists, and can be countered only by including in training programs consideration for the total range of training needs. But perhaps this is not too serious a tendency, at least for a while, if it is true that training in sensitivity to human relations has been so long neglected that there is a large gap to be made up.

In adding up the accomplishments of group dynamics to date it seems clear that the record is impressive. It has opened up new vistas of human potentiality that give promise of bringing about a social technology that will produce even greater miracles than those wrought by the material technology developed over the last century. It has accumulated massive bodies of knowledge—more than we yet know how to use.

Important as have been the discoveries to date, it seems obvious to us that the surface has only been scratched. The years ahead are bound to bring further exciting developments, both in pushing back the frontiers of knowledge about human relations and in applying these unlocked secrets to practical human affairs. We look forward to an increasingly thrilling adventure in exploring new territories with the social scientists. And we hope our readers will join us on the trip.

Chapter 6

READINGS FOR FURTHER UNDERSTANDING

THE BOOKS, PAMPHLETS, and periodicals listed below do not constitute an exhaustive bibliography of group dynamics literature. Rather, they have been selected to provide (1) a general overview of group dynamics theory, (2) representative examples of the different approaches to research, and (3) some illustrative samplings of practical application. We hope our annotations will help you to find the kind of help you want in your quest for further understanding.

Books

ADORNO, T. W., FRENKEL-BRUNSWIK, ELSE, DEVINSON, DANIEL, and SANFORD, R. N. *The Authoritarian Personality*. New York: Harper & Brothers, 1950. 990 pp. An analysis of research about social discrimination based on a sociopsychological approach. The central theme is a new concept—the rise of an "anthropological" species the authors call the authoritarian type of man.

BALES, R. F. *Interaction Process Analysis: A Method for the Study of Small Groups*. Cambridge: Addison-Wesley Publishing Company, Inc. 1950. 203 pp. A comprehensive report of the development of a category system for interaction observation.

BARNARD, CHESTER. *Functions of the Executive*. Cambridge: Harvard University Press, 1938. 334 pp. A theory of formal organization.

BENNE, KENNETH, and MUNTYAN, BOZIDAR. *Human Relations in Curriculum Change*. New York: Dryden Press, 1951. 363 pp. A collection of articles on conceptual tools for analyzing change-situations, group methods in curriculum change, democratic ethics and the management of change, and leadership in curriculum change.

CARTWRIGHT, DORWIN, and ZANDER, ALVIN, eds. *Group Dynamics Research and Theory*. Evanston, Ill.: Row, Peterson & Co., 1953. 642 pp. A comprehensive collection of reports and articles on the methods and findings of research in group dynamics from the various theoretical approaches. Each section contains an introductory chapter by the editors which provides an overview of the theory and findings of that section.

CHASE, STUART. *Roads to Agreement*. New York: Harper & Brothers, 1951. 250 pp. A readable analysis of approaches to the problem of getting agreement, with one chapter on the National Training Laboratories.

COOLEY, C. H. *Social Organization*. New York: Charles Scribner's Sons, 1909. 426 pp. A classic, early speculative statement on the importance of the analysis of informal structure and the primary group.

COYLE, GRACE, ed. *Studies in Group Behavior*. New York: Harper & Brothers, 1937. 258 pp. Case studies of five club groups according to the social group work approach.

FRANK, LAWRENCE K. *How to Be a Modern Leader*. New York: Association Press, 1954. 62 pp. An interpretative analysis of the implications of research in group dynamics for personal leadership.

GIBB, J. R., PLATTS, G. N., and MILLER, L. F. *Dynamics of Participative Groups*. St. Louis: John S. Swift Co., 1951. 81 pp. A discussion of the problems of applying group dynamics.

GOULDNER, ALVIN W., ed. *Studies in Leadership*. New York:

Harper & Brothers, 1950. 736 pp. A collection of articles on leadership by social scientists of various disciplines, giving a comprehensive picture of the status of speculation about leadership in 1950.

GUETZKOW, HAROLD, ed. *Groups, Leadership and Men.* Pittsburgh: Carnegie Press, 1951. 293 pp. Reports on basic research sponsored by the Office of Naval Research between 1945 and 1950, including research in group behavior, leadership, and individual behaviors.

HARE, PAUL, BORGATTA, E. F., and BALES, R. F. *Small Groups: Studies in Social Interaction.* New York: Alfred A. Knopf, Inc., 1955. 666 pp. A collection of statements of theory and reports of research on small groups, with emphasis on studies using the interaction analysis approach. Contains an especially comprehensive annotated bibliography.

HOMANS, GEORGE C. *The Human Group.* New York: Harcourt, Brace and Company, 1950. 484 pp. A classic description of the interaction-analysis approach applied to groups ranging from a family in Tikopia to a modern factory.

JENNINGS, HELEN H. *Leadership and Isolation.* New York: Longmans, Green & Co., Inc., 1950 (2nd ed.). 349 pp. A study of social structure and personality using the sociometric approach.

KNOWLES, MALCOLM, and KNOWLES, HULDA. *How to Develop Better Leaders.* New York: Association Press, 1955. 64 pp. A manual for applying group dynamics findings to the training of leaders, with suggestions for organizing and conducting various kinds of leadership training programs.

LEWIN, KURT. *Field Theory in Social Science.* Dorwin Cartwright, ed. New York: Harper & Brothers, 1951. 346 pp. Selected papers by Lewin explaining the ideas and methods underlying the field theoretical approach. Very technical.

———. *Resolving Social Conflicts*, Gertrud Weiss Lewin, ed. New York: Harper & Brothers, 1948. 230 pp. A collection of papers by Lewin dealing with problems of changing culture, conflicts in face-to-face groups, intergroup conflicts, and belongingness.

LINDEMAN, EDUARD C. *Social Education.* New York: New Republic, 1933. 233 pp. A report on the processes used by small deliberate committees and conferences in the solution of large social problems in "The Inquiry."

LIPPITT, RONALD. *Training in Community Relations.* New York: Harper & Brothers, 1949. 286 pp. A report of a pioneer program of human relations training and action-research, conducted in Connecticut in 1946.

————, Watson, Joanne, and Westley, Bruce. *The Dynamics of Planned Change.* New York: Harcourt, Brace and Company, 1958. 312 pp. A formulation of a general theory of change based on the field theoretical approach.

MAIER, NORMAN R. F. *Principles of Human Relations.* New York: John Wiley & Sons, Inc., 1952. 474 pp. A discussion of problems of human relations in industry, new techniques and approach to them, and the training of persons in effective techniques.

MILES, MATTHEW B. *Learning to Work in Groups.* New York: Bureau of Publications, Teachers College, Columbia University, 1959. 285 pp. A clear and comprehensive statement of principles of applied group dynamics, with specific helps for designing training programs, assuming the trainer's role, evaluating training programs, and organizing training activities (with instructions for 115 training exercises).

MORENO, J. L. *Who Shall Survive?* Beacon, N. Y.: Beacon House, 1953 (rev. ed.). 763 pp. A classic statement of the sociometric approach.

ROETHLISBERGER, F. J., and DICKSON, W. J. *Management and the Worker.* Cambridge: Harvard University Press, 1939. 615 pp. A comprehensive presentation of the classic Western Electric studies.

ROGERS, CARL R. *Client-Centered Therapy.* Boston: Houghton Mifflin Company, 1951. 560 pp. An explanation of the nondirective approach to therapy, with a chapter on "Group-Centered Leadership and Administration."

ROSS, MURRAY G., and HENDRY, CHARLES E. *New Under-*

standings of Leadership. New York: Association Press, 1957. 158 pp. A survey of research on leadership, and a statement of the implications of the research for leaders and leadership development. An eclectic approach.

SCHEIDLINGER, SAUL. *Psychoanalysis and Group Behavior.* New York: W. W. Norton & Company, Inc., 1952. 245 pp. An interpretation of Freudian group psychology and its implications, especially for education, social group work, and group psychotherapy.

STOCK, DOROTHY, and THELEN, HERBERT A. *Emotional Dynamics and Group Culture.* Washington: National Training Laboratories, 1958. 296 pp. A report of research on the emotional factors at work in groups, based on the theoretical concepts of W. R. Bion.

SULLIVAN, DOROTHEA F., ed. *Readings in Group Work.* New York: Association Press, 1952. 438 pp. A collection of articles from a variety of publications dealing with the application of knowledge about groups to social group work.

THELEN, HERBERT A. *Dynamics of Groups at Work.* Chicago: The University of Chicago Press, 1954. 379 pp. Part I analyzes six kinds of group activities: citizen action, classroom teaching, faculty in-service training, administration and management, the laboratory method of human relations training, and public meetings. Part II discusses concepts which are relevant to all groups: membership, integration, evaluating and acting, factors in the problem-solving situation, control, leadership, community.

Pamphlets

Adult Education Association of the U.S.A., 743 North Wabash Avenue, Chicago 11, Illinois. *Leadership Pamphlets,* especially No. 1, "How to Lead Discussions"; No. 2, "Planning Better Programs"; No. 4, "Understanding How Groups Work"; No. 6, "How to Use Role Playing"; No. 8, "Training Group Leaders"; and No. 11, "Conferences That Work." Also, Leaders' Digests Nos. 1, 2, and 3.

National Education Association, Division of Adult Education Services, 1201 Sixteenth Street, N.W., Washington 6, D. C.:

"Educational Dynamics: Theory and Research," by Herbert A. Thelen.

"Explorations in Human Relations Training: An Assessment of Experience, 1947-1952." A six-year report of the National Training Laboratories.

"My Group and I" by Gordon Lippitt and Warren Schmidt.

"Report of the Summer Laboratory Sessions" for 1955, 1956, 1957, and 1958.

Beacon House, P. O. Box 311, Beacon, N. Y.:

Sociometry Monographs, especially No. 3, "Sociometric Measurements of Social Configurations" by J. L. Moreno and Helen H. Jennings; No. 14, "Sociometry and Leadership" by H. H. Jennings; and No. 20, "Sociometry, 1937-1947: Theory and Methods" by C. P. Loomis, J. A. Beegle, and T. W. Longmore.

Psychodrama Monographs, especially No. 9, "Reality Practice in Education" by Alvin Zander, Ronald Lippitt, and Charles E. Hendry.

Periodicals

Adult Leadership. Published monthly except July and August by the Adult Education Association, 743 North Wabash Avenue, Chicago 11, Illinois. Contains practical articles and reports of experience.

The Group. Incorporated in 1955 into *Social Work.* National Association of Social Workers, One Park Avenue, New York 16, N. Y. Official organ of the social work profession.

Group Psychotherapy. Published quarterly by the American Society of Group Psychotherapy and Psychodrama, Beacon House, P. O. Box 311, Beacon, N. Y. Emphasizes group research in psychotherapy.

Human Relations. Published quarterly by the Research Center for Group Dynamics, University of Michigan, Ann

Arbor, Michigan (in collaboration with the Tavistock Clinic, London, England). Contains technical reports of scientific research from a variety of approaches.

Journal of Social Issues. Published quarterly by the Society for the Psychological Study of Social Issues, Association Press, 291 Broadway, New York 7, N. Y. Reports of basic and applied research in various topical areas.

Sociometry. Published quarterly by the American Sociological Society, New York University, Washington Square, New York 3, N. Y. Contains reports of research and theoretical articles of the sociometric approach.

Bibliographies

In addition to the bibliographies on group dynamics that appear in most of the books cited above, the following listings are especially comprehensive:

Benne, Kenneth D., and Levit, Grace, "The Nature of Groups and Helping Groups Improve their Operation," *Review of Educational Research*, XXIII, No. 4 (October, 1953), 305-308.

Horwitz, Murray, "The Conceptual Status of Group Dynamics," *Review of Educational Research*, XXIII, No. 4 (October, 1954), 323-328.

Shils, E. A., "The Study of the Primary Group," in D. Lerner and H. D. Laswell, eds., *The Policy Sciences*. Stanford University Press, 1951, pp. 44-69.

Strodtbeck, F. L., and Hare, A. P., "Bibliography of Small Group Research (From 1900 Through 1953)," *Sociometry*, 1954, XVII, 107-178.

NOTES BY CHAPTERS

Chapter 1. What Is Group Dynamics?

1. Kurt Lewin, *Field Theory in Social Science*, Dorwin Cartwright, ed. (New York: Harper & Brothers, 1951), p. 169.
2. Paul Hare, Edgar Borgatta, and Robert Bales, *Small Groups* (New York: Alfred A. Knopf, Inc., 1955), pp. 2-3. By permission.
3. Kenneth D. Benne and Grace Levit, "The Nature of Groups and Helping Groups Improve Their Operation," *Review of Educational Research* (published by American Educational Research Association, Washington 6, D.C.), XXIII, No. 4 (October, 1953), p. 290. By permission
4. Alvin W. Gouldner, *Studies in Leadership* (New York: Harper & Brothers, 1950), p. 25.
5. Dorwin Cartwright and Alvin Zander, *Group Dynamics Research and Theory* (Evanston, Ill.: Row, Peterson & Company, 1953), p. 4. By permission.
6. Kurt Lewin, *Field Theory in Social Science*, Dorwin Cartwright, ed. (New York: Harper & Brothers, 1951), p. 63. By permission.
7. Raymond B. Cattell, "New Concepts for Measuring Leadership in Terms of Group Syntality," *Human Relations*, 1951, VI, 163.

8. Ruth Strang, "Some Progress Has Been Made," *Readings in Group Work*, Dorothea F. Sullivan, ed. (New York: Association Press, 1952), p. 215.

Chapter 2. Understanding Individual Behavior

1. Dorothy Stock and Herbert A. Thelen, *Emotional Dynamics and Group Culture* (Washington 6, D.C.: National Training Laboratories, 1958), pp. 22-23. By permission.

Chapter 3. Understanding Group Behavior

1. Kenneth D. Benne and Paul Sheats, "Functional Roles of Group Members," *Journal of Social Issues*, Vol. IV, No. 2, Spring, 1948, p. 41.
2. Murray G. Ross and Charles E. Hendry, *New Understandings of Leadership* (New York: Association Press, 1957), p. 36. By permission.
3. See Harold Guetzkow, *Groups, Leadership and Men* (Pittsburgh: Carnegie Press, 1951).
4. Based on Cartwright and Zander, *op. cit.*, p. 141.
5. Based on *Ibid.*, p. 305.

Chapter 4. Practical Applications

1. Herbert A. Thelen, *Dynamics of Groups at Work* (Chicago: University of Chicago Press, 1954), p. 181. Copyright 1954 by The University of Chicago. All rights reserved. By permission.
2. Leland P. Bradford, "An Approach to Human Relations Training," *Report of the Eleventh Summer Laboratory Sessions, Bethel, Maine, 1957* (Washington 6, D.C.: National Training Laboratories, 1957).
3. *Ibid.*

4. Herbert A. Thelen, *Dynamics of Groups at Work, op. cit.*, p. 191. Reprinted by permission of The University of Chicago Press.
5. The process of "group self-training" is described in the authors' previous book, *How to Develop Better Leaders* (New York: Association Press, 1955), p. 17.

INDEX